delicious.
Simple

Welcome

With so many of us living such busy lives these days, trying to juggle lots of different things at once, dinner sometimes just has to be a no-fuss affair – but that doesn't mean that we need to compromise on flair or flavour.

Simple will show you how to put together a delicious supper in no time at all. Just keep a few pantry staples on hand, such as pasta, rice or couscous, and match them with a handful of fresh ingredients. It's as simple as that.

Valli

Contents

Seafood

Vegetarian

Orecchiette with hot-smoked salmon, peas & beurre blanc sauce

400g orecchiette or other
short dried pasta
1 cup (120g) frozen peas
250g hot-smoked salmon
or trout fillets, skin
removed, flaked
2 tbs thickened cream
2 tbs chopped dill, plus extra
sprigs to serve

Buerre blanc sauce
⅓ cup (80ml) white wine
⅓ cup (80ml) white wine
vinegar
2 eschalots, finely chopped
175g chilled unsalted butter,
chopped

Cook pasta in a saucepan of boiling salted water according to packet instructions. Drain, reserving ¼ cup (60ml) cooking liquid.

Meanwhile, to make beurre blanc sauce, place wine, vinegar and eschalot in a saucepan over medium-low heat. Cook for 3–4 minutes until liquid is reduced to 1 tablespoon. Whisking constantly, add the butter, 1 piece at a time, until mixture is thick. Remove from heat and cover to keep warm.

Blanch peas in boiling salted water for 1 minute. Refresh under cold running water, then drain.

Combine pasta with the beurre blanc sauce in a serving bowl, adding a little of the reserved cooking liquid to loosen, if necessary. Add peas, salmon, cream and dill, and gently toss to combine. Serve with the extra sprigs dill. **Serves 4**

Wild mushroom & truffle orzotto

1 tbs olive oil

20g unsalted butter

500g mixed mushrooms (such as Swiss brown, button and flat mushrooms), sliced

½ cup (125ml) dry white wine

1 cup (250ml) chicken stock

400g orzo (risoni) pasta

2 tbs truffle butter* or truffle oil*

2 tbs chopped flat-leaf parsley

Grated parmesan or slices of ripe brie or Taleggio cheese*, to serve

Heat the oil and butter in a large frypan over high heat. Add the mushrooms and cook, stirring occasionally, for 3 minutes or until wilted and starting to brown. Reduce the heat to medium, add the wine and simmer for 2–3 minutes until all the wine is absorbed. Add the stock and cook, stirring occasionally, for 15 minutes or until most of the liquid has been absorbed.

Meanwhile, cook the pasta in a saucepan of boiling salted water according to packet instructions. Drain.

Stir the truffle butter or oil and parsley into the mushroom mixture and season well with sea salt and pepper. Add the pasta and stir well to combine, then divide among bowls and serve topped with parmesan, brie or Taleggio. **Serves 4**

* Truffle butter, truffle oil and Taleggio (an Italian washed-rind cheese) are available from gourmet food shops and delis.

Spaghetti with mussels

¼ cup (60ml) extra virgin
   olive oil
1 long red chilli, seeds
   removed, finely chopped
4 garlic cloves, finely
   chopped
1 onion, finely chopped
1 baby fennel, finely chopped
¾ cup (185ml) dry white wine
400g can chopped tomatoes
1kg pot-ready mussels
400g spaghetti
¼ cup chopped flat-leaf
   parsley
1 tbs grated lemon zest,
   plus lemon halves to serve

Heat the oil in a large saucepan over medium heat. Add the chilli, garlic, onion and fennel, then cook, stirring, for 15 minutes or until softened. Add the wine to the pan and bring to a simmer. Stir in the tomato and cook for 3–4 minutes until slightly reduced. Add the mussels, then cover with a lid. Cook, shaking the pan occasionally, for 2 minutes. Remove opened mussels and set aside. Cook for a further 2 minutes, then discard any mussels that remain closed. Return the opened mussels to the pan and season to taste.

Meanwhile, cook the spaghetti in a large saucepan of boiling salted water according to the packet instructions, then drain.

Add the spaghetti to the sauce and toss to combine. Scatter with the parsley and lemon zest. Serve with lemon halves. **Serves 4–6**

Fettuccine with sausage & peas

400g pork and herb
   sausages, casing removed
2 tbs chopped mint, plus
   extra leaves to garnish
2 cups (240g) frozen peas
250g mascarpone cheese
Juice of 1 lemon
2 tbs olive oil
500g fettuccine
⅔ cup (50g) grated parmesan

Combine the sausage meat and mint in a bowl. Roll into about 24 small (3cm) meatballs and chill until needed.

Cook the peas in a pan of boiling salted water for 1–2 minutes until tender. Drain, then return to the pan and crush with a fork.

Stir in mascarpone and lemon juice, then season and set aside.

Heat the olive oil in a frypan over medium heat. Add the meatballs in batches if necessary, and cook, turning, for 3–4 minutes until browned all over and cooked through.

Meanwhile, cook the pasta according to packet instructions. Drain, reserving 1 cup (250ml) of the cooking water.

Add the pasta and pea mixture to the meatball pan with enough of the reserved water to form a sauce, then toss briefly to combine and heat through. Stir in half the parmesan. Divide among bowls, then serve topped with extra mint and remaining parmesan.

Serves 4

DPS (daily pasta special)

2 tbs olive oil

4 garlic cloves, finely
chopped

1 small red chilli, seeds
removed, finely chopped

4 anchovy fillets, drained,
chopped

20 basil leaves, chopped,
plus extra leaves to garnish

1 cup (160g) pitted kalamata
olives, chopped

2 tbs baby capers, rinsed

2 tbs tomato paste

600ml tomato passata (sugo)*

500g fettuccine

Extra virgin olive oil, to serve

Grated parmesan, to serve
(optional)

Heat the oil in a frypan over medium heat. Add the garlic, chilli, anchovy and basil and cook, stirring, for 1 minute or until fragrant. Add the olives, capers, tomato paste and passata and simmer, stirring occasionally, for 10 minutes until thickened.

Meanwhile, cook the pasta in a saucepan of boiling salted water according to packet instructions. Drain, then divide among serving dishes. Spoon over the sauce, garnish with extra basil leaves and drizzle with extra virgin olive oil. Serve with parmesan, if desired.

Serves 4

* Tomato passata is available in bottles from supermarkets and greengrocers.

Rigatoni with spicy sausage sauce

1 onion, chopped

1 carrot, chopped

1 celery stalk, chopped

4 garlic cloves, chopped

1 tbs oregano leaves,
plus extra to serve

½ tsp dried chilli flakes

2 tbs olive oil

500g Italian pork sausages,
casings removed

500g lean pork mince

1 tbs tomato paste

200ml red wine

2 x 400g cans chopped
tomatoes

½ cup chopped
flat-leaf parsley

500g rigatoni or other
short dried pasta

Shaved parmesan, to serve

Place onion, carrot, celery, garlic, oregano and chilli flakes in a food processor and whiz until finely chopped. Set aside.

Heat oil in a large saucepan over medium-high heat. Add sausage meat and mince, then cook, breaking up lumps with a wooden spoon, for 3–4 minutes until browned. Remove with a slotted spoon and set aside.

Add vegetable mixture to pan and cook, stirring, for 2–3 minutes until starting to soften. Add tomato paste and cook for 1 minute. Stir in the wine, then return meat to pan with the tomato and parsley. Bring to a simmer, then cook, partially covered, stirring occasionally, for 1 hour or until reduced. Remove from heat.

Meanwhile, cook pasta in a saucepan of boiling salted water according to packet instructions. Drain, reserving ½ cup (125ml) cooking liquid.

Add pasta to sauce and toss to combine, adding a little reserved cooking liquid to loosen the sauce, if necessary. Season with sea salt and freshly ground black pepper, and serve with shaved parmesan and extra oregano. **Serves 4–6**

Pasta genovese

12 slices flat pancetta*
400g maccheroni al ferretto*
   or other short pasta
3 large kipfler potatoes
   (about 400g), peeled,
   cut into 1cm-thick slices
200g green beans, trimmed
1 cup (120g) frozen peas
Shaved parmesan, to serve

Pesto

2 cups firmly packed
   basil leaves
⅓ cup (50g) pine nuts
2 garlic cloves
1¼ cups (100g) grated
   parmesan
150ml extra virgin olive oil

Preheat the oven to 200°C. Line a baking tray with baking paper.

Arrange the pancetta in a single layer on the lined tray. Bake for 8–10 minutes until crispy. Cool for 5 minutes, then break into large pieces.

Meanwhile, for the pesto, place the basil, nuts, garlic and parmesan in a food processor and whiz until combined. With the motor running, add the oil in a slow, steady stream until a smooth paste. Set aside. (The pesto will keep in the refrigerator in a jar under a thin layer of olive oil for up to 1 week.)

Cook the pasta in a large saucepan of salted boiling water according to the packet instructions, adding the potato for the final 8 minutes and the beans and peas for the final 1 minute of cooking time, until the pasta is al dente and the vegetables are tender. Drain the pasta and vegetables, reserving the cooking water.

Toss the pasta and vegetables with the pesto, adding enough reserved cooking water so the pesto coats the pasta. Serve the pasta topped with the crispy pancetta and shaved parmesan.
Serves 4

* Flat pancetta and maccheroni al ferretto are available from delis.

Secret ingredient bolognese sauce

1 carrot, chopped

1 onion, chopped

1 celery stalk, chopped

6 thin slices pancetta,
  chopped

2 tbs rosemary leaves

2 garlic cloves, chopped

1 tbs olive oil

500g beef mince

1 tbs tomato paste

1 cup (250ml) red wine

400g can chopped tomatoes

1 cup (250ml) tomato passata
  (sugo)*

1 cup (250ml) beef stock

1 small red chilli, seeds
  removed, finely chopped

30g dark chocolate (70%
  cocoa solids), grated

500g tagliatelle or other long
  dried pasta

Grated parmesan and basil
  leaves, to serve

Place carrot, onion, celery, pancetta, rosemary and garlic in a food processor and process until finely chopped.

Heat oil in a large saucepan over medium-high heat. Add vegetable mixture and cook, stirring, for 5 minutes or until softened. Add mince and cook, breaking up lumps with a wooden spoon, for 3–4 minutes until browned. Add tomato paste and cook for 1 minute, then add wine and cook for 5 minutes or until liquid is reduced by half. Add canned tomato, passata and stock, then season with sea salt and freshly ground black pepper. Cover, reduce heat to low, then cook for 1 hour. Remove lid and cook for a further 30 minutes or until reduced and thickened. Add chilli for the last 5 minutes of cooking. Remove saucepan from heat, add chocolate and stir to combine.

Meanwhile, cook pasta in a large saucepan of boiling salted water according to packet instructions. Drain, then add to sauce and toss to combine. Serve topped with grated parmesan and basil. **Serves 6**

* Tomato passata is available in bottles from supermarkets and greengrocers.

Spaghetti carbonara

1 tbs olive oil

20g unsalted butter

100g sliced pancetta, cut into
   thin strips

2 garlic cloves, finely
   chopped

400g spaghetti

3 eggs

150ml pure (thin) cream

⅔ cup (50g) grated parmesan

⅔ cup (50g) grated pecorino
   cheese

2 tbs chopped flat-leaf
   parsley

Heat the oil and butter in a frypan over medium-high heat. Add the pancetta and cook, stirring, for 3–4 minutes until starting to crisp. Stir in garlic, then remove from the heat and set aside.

Cook the pasta in a large saucepan of boiling salted water according to packet instructions. Meanwhile, beat the eggs and cream together in a bowl, then season with salt and pepper.

Drain the pasta, reserving ½ cup (125ml) of the cooking water, then return to the saucepan off the heat. Quickly add the egg and pancetta mixtures and toss to coat the pasta. Add half each of the parmesan, pecorino and parsley, then toss to combine (the residual heat from the pasta will cook the egg).

Divide the pasta among warm bowls, then serve topped with the remaining cheese and parsley. **Serves 4**

Macadamia-crumbed chicken strips

½ cup (75g) macadamias,
  roughly chopped
2 cups (100g) panko
  breadcrumbs*
1 cup (150g) plain flour
2 eggs, lightly beaten
12 chicken tenderloins or
  4 x 170g chicken breast
  fillets, cut into thirds
  lengthways
Sunflower oil, to deep-fry

Tomato salsa
4 tomatoes, seeds removed,
  chopped
1 red onion, chopped
1 long green chilli, seeds
  removed, chopped
1 tbs grated ginger
2 tbs chopped coriander,
  plus extra leaves to serve
Juice of 1 lime, plus
  lime wedges to serve
⅓ cup (80ml) extra virgin
  olive oil

For the tomato salsa, place all the ingredients in a bowl, season, then toss to combine. Set aside.

Place the macadamias and breadcrumbs in a food processor and whiz to fine crumbs. Transfer to a bowl.

Place the flour in a separate bowl and season. Place the egg in a third bowl.

Dip the chicken first in flour, shaking off the excess, then in the egg and finally in the macadamia crumbs, making sure each piece is well coated. Chill for 20 minutes to firm up.

Preheat the oven to 150°C.

Half fill a large saucepan or deep-fryer with the oil and heat to 190°C (if you don't have a kitchen thermometer, a cube of bread dropped into the oil will turn golden after 30 seconds when the oil is hot enough). In batches, deep-fry the crumbed chicken strips for 3–4 minutes until golden and cooked through. Remove with a slotted spoon and drain on paper towel. Transfer to a baking tray and keep warm in the oven while you cook the remaining chicken.

Serve the chicken strips with the tomato salsa, lime wedges and extra coriander leaves. **Serves 4**

* Panko are light, crunchy Japanese breadcrumbs, available from Asian food shops and selected supermarkets.

Crockpot-au-feu

1.6kg free-range chicken
1 large onion, chopped
1 bouquet garni*
1 cup (250ml) white wine
1 cup (250ml) chicken stock
4 baby leeks, trimmed
1 bunch baby (Dutch) carrots,
   ends trimmed
4 potatoes, peeled, chopped
100g thin green beans, ends
   trimmed
Chopped flat-leaf parsley,
   to sprinkle
Sliced toasted baguette and
   fresh ricotta, to serve

Season the chicken and truss with string. Place the chicken and onion in a slow cooker. Add the bouquet garni, wine, stock and enough water to cover. Season with salt and pepper and cover with the lid. Cook on a low heat for 6–8 hours until the chicken is tender and cooked. Add the leek, carrot and potato and cook for a further hour, adding the green beans for the final 10 minutes of cooking.

Remove the chicken and slice. Divide the chicken, vegetables and some of the poaching liquid among serving bowls. Season well with salt and pepper and sprinkle with parsley. Serve with toasted baguette and ricotta. **Serves 4**

* To make a bouquet garni, tie together a few bay leaves, parsley sprigs and thyme sprigs with kitchen string.

Warm spiced quinoa & chicken salad

2 tbs olive oil

6 skinless chicken thigh fillets,
  cut into 2cm pieces

1 onion, finely chopped

2 garlic cloves, finely
  chopped

1 tbs grated ginger

1 long green chilli, seeds
  removed, finely chopped

1 tbs panch phoran*

2 tsp mild curry powder

2 cups (400g) quinoa

2 cups (500ml) chicken stock

1 cup (120g) frozen peas,
  blanched, drained

1½ cups finely
  chopped coriander

Micro herbs (such as
  amaranth*, optional),
  to garnish

Thick Greek-style yoghurt
  and pappadums, to serve

Heat 1 tablespoon oil in a large frypan over high heat. Brown half the chicken for 2 minutes each side or until golden, then set aside. Repeat with remaining 1 tablespoon oil and chicken.

Reduce heat to medium-high, add onion to same pan and cook, stirring, for 3–4 minutes until softened. Add garlic, ginger, chilli, panch phoran and curry powder, stir for 1 minute or until fragrant, then add quinoa and stock. Return chicken and any cooking juices to the pan, bring to a simmer, then reduce heat to low and cook for 20 minutes or until chicken is cooked and liquid absorbed. Stir through peas and coriander, scatter over micro herbs, if using, and serve warm or at room temperature with yoghurt and pappadums.
Serves 4–6

* Panch phoran is an Indian spice blend that includes cumin, fenugreek and fennel, available from spice shops, Indian food shops and online at herbies.com.au (substitute brown mustard seeds). Amaranth, a ruby-red edible plant whose seeds are used in similar ways to quinoa, is available from specialty greengrocers.

Duck & pineapple red curry

1 tbs peanut oil

8 spring onions (white part only), sliced on an angle

2 garlic cloves, finely chopped

1 lemongrass stem, halved

3 tbs red curry paste

1 Chinese barbecued duck*, chopped

400ml coconut milk

450g can pineapple pieces in natural juice, drained

3 kaffir lime leaves*

2 tsp brown sugar

2 tsp fish sauce

½ bunch coriander leaves, chopped, plus whole leaves to serve

Steamed rice and lime wedges, to serve

Heat oil in a wok over high heat. Add the spring onion, garlic, lemongrass and curry paste and stir-fry for 1 minute or until fragrant. Add the duck, coconut milk, pineapple, 2 kaffir lime leaves and chopped coriander. Bring to the boil, then reduce the heat to medium and simmer for 10 minutes or until the duck is warmed through and the sauce has reduced slightly. Add brown sugar and fish sauce to taste.

Finely shred the remaining kaffir lime leaf. Serve the curry, garnished with shredded kaffir lime and coriander leaves, with rice and lime wedges. **Serves 6–8**

* Barbecued duck is available from Chinese barbecue shops and restaurants; ask them to chop the duck for you. Kaffir lime leaves are available from Asian food shops and greengrocers.

Chicken pesto pies

40g unsalted butter

1 leek (white part only), thinly
sliced

6 button mushrooms, sliced

2 tbs plain flour

¾ cup (185ml) chicken stock

¾ cup (185ml) thickened
cream

2 tbs good-quality basil
pesto* plus extra to serve
if desired

3 cups (480g) chopped
cooked chicken

6 large, ready-made
vol-au-vent cases*

2 sheets frozen puff pastry,
thawed

1 egg, lightly beaten

1 tsp nigella seeds* or sesame
seeds (optional)

250g vine-ripened cherry
tomatoes

1 tbs olive oil

Preheat the oven to 180°C.

Melt the butter in a pan over medium-low heat. Add the leek and cook, stirring, for 5 minutes or until soft. Add the mushroom and cook for a further minute, then add the flour and stir for 1 minute. Gradually stir in the chicken stock, then bring the mixture to simmer. Add the cream and cook for 2–3 minutes, stirring, until thickened. Allow to cool, season, then stir in pesto. Stir the chicken into the sauce.

Using a vol-au-vent as a template, cut 6 lids from the puff pastry sheets. Place the vol-au-vents on a baking tray and fill with the chicken mixture. Brush the edges of the pastry lids with a little water and place on top, pressing the edges to seal. Brush the tops of the pies with the beaten egg and sprinkle with nigella seeds, if using. Bake for 15–20 minutes until golden.

Meanwhile, place the tomatoes on a tray, drizzle with the olive oil and season. Bake in the oven with the pies for 6–8 minutes until the tomatoes are just starting to burst. Serve the pies with the tomatoes and extra pesto, if desired. **Makes 6**

* Good-quality pesto is available from delis; or see recipe, p 18. Vol-au-vent pastries are available from the baking section in supermarkets. Nigella seeds are available from delis and Asian food shops.

Chicken paella

1 tbs olive oil

1 onion, finely chopped

2 chorizo sausages, peeled,
   sliced

3 streaky bacon rashers, rind
   removed, sliced into batons

2 cups (400g) calasparra*
   or arborio rice

1 tbs sundried tomato paste

280g jar chargrilled capsicum
   strips*, drained

3 tomatoes, seeds removed,
   chopped

3 garlic cloves, crushed

2 tsp smoked paprika
   (pimenton)

¼ tsp saffron threads

6 cups (1.5L) chicken stock

¾ cup (185ml) dry white wine

1 barbecued chicken, cut into
   portions

1 tbs chopped flat-leaf
   parsley

Heat the olive oil in a large, deep frypan over medium heat. Add the onion, chorizo and bacon and cook, stirring, for 5–6 minutes until onion is soft and bacon is starting to crisp. Add the rice, stirring to coat in the mixture. Add the tomato paste, capsicum, tomato, garlic and paprika, then cook, stirring, for 2–3 minutes.

Add saffron, chicken stock and wine, then bring to the boil.

Simmer gently, uncovered, stirring occasionally, for 15 minutes or until the liquid is evaporated and the rice is just cooked.

Meanwhile, cut the chicken meat into bite-sized chunks. Stir into the paella and cook for a further 2–3 minutes until heated through. Season to taste, then stir through parsley and serve. **Serves 4–6**

* Chargrilled capsicum is available from supermarkets. Calasparra rice is available from delis and gourmet food shops.

Easy coq au vin

8 eschalots, peeled

1 tbs olive oil

60g sliced pancetta, cut into
strips

8 chicken thigh fillets, cut into
3cm pieces

2 tbs plain flour

3 garlic cloves, finely
chopped

150g button mushrooms,
quartered

2 tbs tomato paste

1 cup (250ml) good-quality
chicken stock or chicken
consommé

1 cup (250ml) dry red wine

1 tbs chopped fresh thyme
leaves

2 bay leaves

Chopped flat-leaf parsley and
sliced toasted baguette,
to serve

Par-cook the eschalots in boiling water for 5 minutes, then drain and set aside.

Heat the oil in a large deep frypan or casserole pan over medium heat. Add pancetta and cook, stirring, for 2–3 minutes until starting to crisp. Season chicken, then add to the pan and cook for 5–6 minutes until lightly browned. Add flour and stir to coat chicken, then stir in the garlic, mushrooms and tomato paste.

Once everything is well combined, add the stock, wine, thyme, bay leaves and eschalots. Season well, bring to the boil, then reduce heat to medium-low and simmer for 20 minutes or until the chicken is cooked through and the sauce has thickened.

Serve the coq au vin in deep bowls with parsley and toasted baguette to mop up the lovely sauce. **Serves 4**

Chicken, tomato & spinach curry

¼ cup (60ml) olive oil

4 garlic cloves, chopped

2 tbs finely grated ginger

2 long red chillies, seeds removed, finely chopped

¼ cup (75g) tikka masala curry paste

6 skinless chicken thigh cutlets

3 potatoes (about 400g), peeled, cut into 3cm cubes

400g can chopped tomatoes

12 fresh curry leaves* (optional)

1 cup (250ml) chicken stock

100g baby spinach leaves

Lime juice, to taste

Pappadams and steamed basmati rice, to serve

Heat the oil in a pan over medium heat. Add the garlic, ginger and chilli, and cook, stirring, for 1–2 minutes until fragrant. Add the curry paste and cook, stirring, for 2–3 minutes until fragrant. Add the chicken, turning to coat in the paste. Cook chicken for 1–2 minutes each side until lightly coloured, then add the potato, tomato, curry leaves and stock. Bring to a simmer, then reduce heat to medium-low, cover and cook for 15 minutes or until the chicken is cooked through and potato is tender.

Remove the lid and cook the curry for a further 20 minutes or until the sauce has thickened. Stir through the spinach and cook for a further 1–2 minutes until spinach has wilted. Add lime juice to taste and season. Serve the curry with pappadams and steamed basmati rice. **Serves 4–6**

* Fresh curry leaves are available from Asian food shops and greengrocers.

Quick Italian-style roast pork

600g desiree potatoes,
  peeled, cut into 3cm
  chunks
2 tbs olive oil
1 rosemary sprig, leaves
  finely chopped
2 garlic cloves, finely
  chopped
2 pork fillets (about 500g
  each), halved
8 thin slices flat pancetta*
250g cherry truss tomatoes,
  separated into sprigs
Good-quality basil pesto*,
  to serve

Preheat the oven to 200°C and grease a large baking tray.

Blanch the potato in boiling salted water for 5 minutes, then drain well. Spread on the tray, toss with 1 tablespoon of oil, then season and roast for 20 minutes.

Meanwhile, mix together the rosemary, garlic and remaining tablespoon of oil. Coat the pork in the mixture, then wrap 2 slices of pancetta around each fillet and secure with kitchen string or toothpicks. Season with salt and pepper. Add the pork to the tray with the potatoes and roast for a further 15 minutes.

Add the tomatoes to the tray, then season and return to the oven for a further 5 minutes until the potato is golden, the pork is cooked and the tomatoes are just starting to soften.

Serve the roast pork and vegetables with pesto to drizzle.

Serves 4

* Flat pancetta is available from selected delis and butchers. Good-quality pesto is available from delis, or see recipe, p 18.

Pork with Caribbean pineapple sauce

4 x 280g pork loin chops
1 tbs olive oil
½ ripe pineapple, peeled,
   cut into 1cm cubes
2 eschalots, finely chopped
2 long red chillies, seeds
   removed, finely chopped
⅓ cup (75g) caster sugar
100ml dark rum
1 tbs red wine vinegar
Steamed snow peas, to serve

Preheat the oven to 170°C.

Season the chops with salt and pepper. Heat the oil in a large frypan over medium-high heat. Add the chops and brown for 2–3 minutes each side, then transfer to a baking tray. Place in the oven and bake for 10 minutes until cooked through.

Meanwhile, return the pan to the heat and add the pineapple, eschalot and chilli. Cook, stirring, for 2–3 minutes until the eschalot has softened. Add the sugar, rum and vinegar and cook, stirring, for 3–4 minutes until the sauce is reduced and sticky.

Divide the pork chops among plates, top with the pineapple sauce and serve with snow peas. **Serves 4**

Frypan pizza

1⅔ cups (250g) self-raising
  flour
¼ cup (60ml) olive oil
1 cup (250ml) good-quality
  pasta sauce
1 ball of fior di latte*
  or 2 bocconcini

Toppings
3 slices prosciutto
6 kalamata olives
Fresh basil leaves

Sift the flour and 1 teaspoon salt into a bowl. Add 2 tablespoons olive oil and ⅓ cup (80ml) water, then mix with your hands to a soft dough that's not too sticky, adding extra flour if necessary. Dust the workbench with flour, then roll out the pastry into a circle to fit a 26cm frypan.

Preheat a grill to high. Heat 1 tablespoon oil in the frypan over low heat. Add the dough and cook for 3–4 minutes until the underside is crisp and golden. Turn and cook on the other side for 2–3 minutes until golden. Spread with the sauce and top with sliced cheese. Place under the grill and cook for 1–2 minutes until the cheese has melted. Scatter with prosciutto, olives and fresh basil, then serve. **Serves 1–2**

* Fior di latte is a fresh cow's milk mozzarella, available from gourmet food shops and delis.

Pork, sage & onion burgers

450g pork sausages
½ packet (100g) sage and
   onion stuffing mix*
1 egg
Olive oil, to brush
4 Turkish rolls or panini, split,
   toasted
Baby spinach or rocket
   leaves, cranberry sauce
   and sour cream, to serve

Remove the sausage casings, then place the sausage meat in a bowl with the stuffing and egg, season, then mix well with your hands. Using damp hands, form the mixture into 4 patties. Cover and chill for 30 minutes.

Preheat the oven to 170°C. Brush a frypan or chargrill pan with oil and heat over medium-high heat. Cook the patties for 2–3 minutes each side until golden. Transfer to a tray, then bake for 5–6 minutes until cooked through. Fill toasted rolls with spinach, patties, cranberry sauce and sour cream. **Serves 4**

* Stuffing mix is available from supermarkets.

Crispy herbed pork cutlets

3 cups panko breadcrumbs*
½ cup (75g) plain flour,
    seasoned
1 tbs fresh lemon thyme
    (or regular thyme) leaves
¾ cup (60g) grated parmesan
3 eggs, beaten
4 pork cutlets
¼ cup (60ml) olive oil
30g unsalted butter
8 sage sprigs
Lemon wedges, to serve

Whiz the breadcrumbs in a food processor with the flour, thyme and parmesan to fine crumbs. Season with salt and pepper, then transfer to a shallow bowl. Place egg in a separate bowl.

Use a meat mallet to lightly pound the eye fillet of each pork cutlet to an even thickness. Dip the pork in the egg, then press into the crumb mixture to coat well all over.

Heat the oil in a large non-stick frypan over medium heat.

Add the pork and fry for 2–3 minutes each side until golden and cooked through. Remove from the pan and set aside. Add the butter and sage sprigs to the pan. When the butter begins to foam, return the pork to the pan and turn to coat in the buttery juices. Serve immediately with lemon wedges. **Serves 4**

* Panko are light, crunchy Japanese breadcrumbs, available from Asian food shops and selected supermarkets.

Pork & olive stew

2 tbs olive oil

2 chorizo sausages, sliced

800g lean diced pork

2 onions, chopped

2 garlic cloves, chopped

1 tsp smoked paprika
(pimenton)*

1 tbs plain flour

¼ cup (60ml) sherry vinegar*
or red wine vinegar

1 cup (250ml) dry sherry

½ cup (125ml) chicken stock

500ml tomato passata (sugo)*

3 thyme sprigs

2 bay leaves

½ cup small Spanish green
olives

2 roasted red capsicums*,
sliced

Torn flat-leaf parsley and
chargrilled bread, to serve

Preheat the oven to 170°C.

Heat 1 tablespoon oil in a large flameproof casserole over medium heat. Add the chorizo and cook for 2–3 minutes until starting to crisp. Remove and set aside. In batches, brown the pork, turning, for 3–4 minutes until sealed on all sides, adding a little more oil if necessary. Remove and set aside with the chorizo.

Add the onion and garlic and cook, stirring, for 2–3 minutes until softened. Stir in the paprika, then return the chorizo and pork to the pan. Stir in the flour, then add the vinegar, sherry, stock, passata, herbs and some salt and pepper, adding a little water to cover the meat if necessary. Bring to a simmer, then cover and transfer to the oven for 1¼ hours.

Add the olives and capsicum, then cover and return to the oven for a further 15 minutes or until the meat is tender and the sauce is reduced. Garnish with parsley and serve with chargrilled bread.
Serves 4

* Smoked paprika and sherry vinegar are available from gourmet food shops and delis. Tomato passata and roasted capsicums are available from delis and selected supermarkets.

Bacon & egg fried rice

¼ cup (60ml) sunflower oil

12 green prawns, peeled, deveined, chopped

1 tbs finely grated lemongrass stem (inner core only)

6 shiitake mushrooms, sliced

4 rashers bacon, rind removed, finely chopped

2 garlic cloves, finely chopped

2 tbs grated ginger

1 small red chilli, seeds removed, finely chopped

1 cup (120g) frozen peas, blanched, refreshed

4 cups cooked jasmine rice

5 spring onions, thinly sliced on the diagonal

¼ cup (60ml) light soy sauce, plus extra to serve

4 quail eggs*

Chilli sauce, to serve

Heat 1 tablespoon sunflower oil in a wok over medium-high heat. Season the prawns, then add to the wok and stir-fry until almost cooked through. Remove the prawns from the wok and set aside.

Add 1 tablespoon oil to the wok. Add the lemongrass, mushroom, bacon, garlic, ginger and chilli, then stir-fry for 2–3 minutes until fragrant and the bacon is crispy. Return the prawns to the wok with the peas and rice, then stir-fry until warmed through. Add the spring onion and soy sauce, toss to combine, then keep warm and set aside.

Add remaining 1 tablespoon oil to a clean, non-stick frypan over medium-high heat. Break the eggs into the pan and fry for 1–2 minutes until the eggwhites are opaque.

Divide the fried rice among 4 serving bowls and place a fried quail egg on top. Serve with a dash of chilli sauce and extra soy sauce. **Serves 4**

* Quail eggs are available from Asian food shops and selected poultry shops.

Spring sausage bake

2 fennel bulbs, trimmed,
  cut into wedges
1 red onion, cut into wedges
2 zucchinis, thickly sliced
1 whole garlic bulb,
  halved horizontally
2 bay leaves
12 good-quality pork
  chipolata sausages
⅓ cup (80ml) olive oil
2 tbs balsamic vinegar
1 tsp chopped thyme leaves
1 tsp chopped rosemary
  leaves
400g mixed small heirloom
  tomatoes* or vine-ripened
  cherry tomatoes, halved
  if large
Good-quality pesto* and basil
  leaves, to serve

Preheat the oven to 200°C.

Place the fennel, onion, zucchini, garlic, bay leaves and sausages in a roasting pan. Drizzle with the olive oil and balsamic vinegar, scatter with the thyme and rosemary, then season.

Bake for 20 minutes, turning once, or until the vegetables are tender. Add the tomatoes to the pan and return to the oven for a further 3–4 minutes until the tomatoes have started to soften and the sausages are cooked through.

Dollop the sausage bake with the pesto and serve scattered with basil leaves. **Serves 4**

* Heirloom tomatoes are available from greengrocers and selected supermarkets. Good-quality basil pesto is available from delis; or see recipe, p 18.

Swedish meatballs

400g pork mince

1 egg

1 onion, grated

1¼ cups (85g) fresh
   breadcrumbs

½ tsp ground allspice

¼ tsp ground cloves

Pinch of nutmeg

1 tbs olive oil

20g unsalted butter

150ml beef stock

2 tbs brown sugar

Lingonberry sauce* or
   cranberry sauce, sour
   cream, dill & parsley
   potatoes, baby cos leaves
   and cucumber slices,
   to serve

Place the mince, egg, onion, breadcrumbs and spices in a food processor, season with salt and pepper and process to combine. With damp hands, form the mixture into 24 walnut-sized balls. Place on a baking tray, cover with plastic wrap and chill in the fridge for 15 minutes to firm up.

Heat the oil and butter in a frypan over medium heat. In batches, cook the meatballs, turning, for 3–4 minutes until golden. Remove from the pan and set aside.

Wipe the frypan clean, then add the stock and sugar. Cook over medium-low heat, stirring, for 3–5 minutes until syrupy.

Return all the meatballs to the pan, coating in the glaze, for a further 1–2 minutes until warmed through. Serve the meatballs with sauce, sour cream, potatoes, lettuce and cucumber. **Makes 24**

* Lingonberry sauce is available from selected delis and Ikea.

Shortcut roast lamb with caramelised onion couscous

3 tsp each of ground cumin, ground coriander and paprika
3 garlic cloves, crushed
⅓ cup (80ml) olive oil
1.5kg easy-carve lamb leg
2 onions, sliced
2 tbs chopped thyme leaves
1½ tbs caster sugar
100ml balsamic vinegar
1 cup (200g) couscous
20g unsalted butter
1 cup (100g) toasted walnuts, chopped
2 tbs chopped flat-leaf parsley
2 tbs walnut oil* or extra virgin olive oil

Preheat the oven to 180°C.

Mix the spices with garlic and 2 tablespoons olive oil. Spread the spice paste all over the lamb, then place in a roasting pan and roast for 1 hour.

Meanwhile, heat the remaining 2 tablespoons olive oil in a frypan over medium-low heat. Add the onion, thyme, 1 teaspoon sea salt and plenty of black pepper. Cook for 4–6 minutes until the onion starts to caramelise. Stir in the sugar and vinegar, decrease the heat to low and cook, stirring occasionally, for 4–5 minutes until almost all the liquid has been absorbed.

Remove lamb from the oven, cover loosely with foil and set aside to rest in a warm place while you make the couscous.

Place the couscous in a bowl and pour over 400ml boiling water. Cover with plastic wrap and stand for 5 minutes. Fluff the couscous grains with a fork, then stir in the caramelised onion, butter, walnuts, parsley and walnut oil. Serve with the roast lamb. **Serves 4–6**

* Walnut oil is available from gourmet food shops.

Greek lamb with orzo

2 tbs olive oil

500g lamb mince

1 onion, finely chopped

4 garlic cloves,
   finely chopped

2 tsp ground cinnamon

1 tsp dried oregano

1½ tsp ground cumin

1½ tsp ground coriander

½ tsp dried chilli flakes

2 x 400g cans chopped
   tomatoes

2 cups (500ml) beef stock

500g orzo (risoni) pasta

Juice of 1 lemon

100g baby spinach leaves

1 cup mint, chopped, plus
   extra leaves to serve

1 cup flat-leaf parsley,
   chopped

¼ cup (40g) pitted kalamata
   olives

½ cup (100g) crumbled feta

Heat 1 tablespoon oil in a large saucepan over medium-high heat. Add lamb and cook, breaking up lumps with a wooden spoon, for 2–3 minutes until browned. Transfer lamb to a plate, draining the fat, and set aside until needed.

Return saucepan to medium heat with the remaining 1 tablespoon oil. Add onion and garlic, and cook, stirring, for 5 minutes or until soft. Add spices and dried herbs, season with sea salt and freshly ground black pepper, then cook, stirring, for 1 minute or until fragrant. Add tomato and stock, bring to a simmer, then cook, uncovered, for 25 minutes. Return the mince to the pan and cook for a further 15 minutes or until the sauce is reduced. Remove from heat.

Meanwhile, cook pasta in a saucepan of boiling salted water according to packet instructions. Drain, reserving ½ cup (125ml) cooking liquid, then return pasta to the pan with lemon juice and toss to combine.

Add the spinach to lamb mixture and toss until wilted, then add mint, parsley and pasta, and toss to combine. Add a little of the reserved liquid if the sauce is too dry.

Serve topped with olives, feta and extra mint leaves. **Serves 4–6**

Egg & meatball shakshouka

¼ cup (60ml) olive oil

1 onion, finely chopped

2 garlic cloves, finely
   chopped

2 tbs good-quality
   red harissa paste*

1 cinnamon quill

2 x 400g cans chopped
   tomatoes

1¼ cups (310ml) beef stock

500g lamb mince

2 tbs chopped coriander, plus
   extra sprigs to serve

100g fresh breadcrumbs

4 eggs

Sliced grilled Turkish bread,
   to serve

Heat 1 tablespoon oil in a frypan over medium heat. Add half the onion and cook for 1–2 minutes, then add half the garlic and 1 tablespoon harissa paste and cook for a further 1–2 minutes until fragrant. Add cinnamon, tomato and stock, stir to combine and season with sea salt and freshly ground black pepper. Reduce heat to medium-low and simmer for 30 minutes.

Meanwhile, combine mince, coriander, breadcrumbs and remaining onion, garlic and 1 tablespoon harissa in a bowl. Season, then form tablespoonfuls of lamb mixture into walnut-sized balls. Refrigerate until ready to cook.

Preheat the oven to 200°C. Heat 1 tablespoon oil over medium heat and cook half the meatballs for 3–4 minutes, turning, until golden all over and almost cooked. Drain on paper towel. Repeat with remaining 1 tablespoon oil and meatballs.

Divide meatballs among 4 x 2-cup (500ml) ovenproof dishes or place in a 1.5L-capacity baking dish, then pour over the hot tomato sauce. Form a well in the centre of each dish and crack an egg into it. If using a large dish, make 4 wells in the tomato mixture. Bake for 8–10 minutes until the eggwhites are just cooked but the yolks are still runny.

Serve with sliced grilled Turkish bread. **Serves 4**

* We used Malouf's Spice Mezza Red Harissa, available from selected delis and gourmet food shops, or online at gregmalouf.com.au and essentialingredient.com.au.

Lamb burgers with tzatziki

1kg lamb mince
1 onion, finely chopped
2 garlic cloves, finely
   chopped
2 tsp ground cumin
1 tsp ground coriander
¼ tsp ground cinnamon
¼ tsp ground allspice
½ tsp dried chilli flakes
2 tbs chopped flat-leaf
   parsley
1 egg
6 sourdough buns, split
2 roasted capsicums*,
   cut into strips

Tzatziki
1 cup (280g) thick Greek-style
   yoghurt
1 Lebanese cucumber, grated
2 garlic cloves, grated
2 tbs chopped mint,
   plus extra leaves to garnish

Place the lamb, onion, garlic, spices, parsley, egg and some salt and pepper in a bowl. Mix with your hands until well combined, then form into 6 patties. Chill for 30 minutes.

For the tzatziki, combine the yoghurt, cucumber, garlic and chopped mint in a bowl. Season, then chill until ready to serve.

Preheat a chargrill pan or barbecue to medium-high heat. Cook the patties for 3–4 minutes each side until cooked through.

Meanwhile, toast the buns, then spread with tzatziki and fill with roast capsicum, lamb patties and extra mint leaves. **Makes 6**

* Roasted capsicums are available from delis.

Lamb & haloumi sausage rolls

500g lamb mince

1 cup (70g) fresh
   breadcrumbs

¼ cup mint jelly

¼ cup finely chopped mint

200g haloumi, grated

2 garlic cloves, finely
   chopped

2 tsp Worcestershire sauce

3 sheets frozen puff pastry,
   thawed

1 egg, lightly beaten

1 tbs nigella seeds

Sliced red onion, mint leaves
   and tomato, to serve

Preheat oven to 180°C. Line a large baking tray with baking paper.

Combine lamb, breadcrumbs, mint jelly, chopped mint, haloumi, garlic and Worcestershire sauce in a bowl. Season with sea salt and freshly ground black pepper. Divide mixture into 6 equal portions, then form each into a long sausage.

Cut each pastry sheet in half. Place a sausage lengthways in the centre of a halved sheet. Brush edges of pastry with a little cold water, then roll up pastry around sausage, sealing edges. Cut each length into 4 sausage rolls, then place, sealed side down, on baking tray. Repeat with remaining pastry and sausage mixture. Brush with beaten egg, then sprinkle over seeds.

Bake for 30 minutes or until puffed and golden. Serve warm with onion, mint and tomato. **Makes 24**

Lamb with curry sauce & Thai basil

400ml coconut milk

2–3 tbs Thai red curry paste
(to taste)

¾ cup (75g) roasted peanuts,
ground, plus extra
chopped to garnish

2 tbs grated palm sugar*

5 kaffir lime leaves*, finely
shredded

¼ cup (60ml) Thai fish sauce

2 x 200g lamb backstraps

1½ tbs sunflower oil

4 Asian red eschalots*, thinly
sliced

1 green chilli, sliced

150g bean sprouts, trimmed

Steamed jasmine rice,
to serve

Juice of 1 lime

1 bunch Thai basil*, leaves
picked

Coriander sprigs, to garnish

Place 200ml of the coconut milk and the curry paste in a wok over medium-high heat and bring to the boil. Add the remaining 200ml coconut milk and simmer for 5 minutes. Add the ground peanuts, sugar, kaffir lime leaves and fish sauce and simmer for 2 minutes, then keep warm over low heat while you cook the lamb.

Season the lamb with salt and pepper. Heat ½ tablespoon oil in a frypan over high heat. Add the lamb and cook, turning to brown on all sides, for 5 minutes for medium-rare (or until done to your liking). Transfer to a plate and cover loosely with foil.

Return the cleaned pan to low heat, then add the remaining oil. Add the eschalot and chilli and cook for 1 minute until softened. Add the bean sprouts and stir for 30 seconds.

Slice the lamb and divide among serving plates with steamed rice. Stir the lime juice into the curry sauce, then spoon over the lamb with the sprout mixture and basil. Garnish with coriander and extra chopped peanuts. **Serves 4**

* Palm sugar, kaffir lime leaves, red eschalots and Thai basil are available from Asian food shops and selected greengrocers.

Gnocchi-topped shepherd's pies

2 tbs olive oil, plus extra
  to toss
100g sliced pancetta or
  bacon, chopped
1 large onion, chopped
2 small carrots, chopped
1 tbs plain flour
4 garlic cloves, chopped
1 tbs tomato paste
1kg lamb mince
1¼ cups (300ml) dry red wine
2 cups (500ml) beef stock
2 bay leaves
2 tsp chopped thyme
2 x 500g packets potato
  gnocchi
40g unsalted butter, melted
2 tbs grated parmesan

Heat the oil in a large frypan over medium heat. Add the pancetta, onion and carrot and cook, stirring, for 5 minutes or until the onion has softened. Add the flour, garlic and tomato paste and cook, stirring, for a further minute. Add the mince and cook for 5–6 minutes until well browned. Add the wine, stock, bay leaves and thyme, season, then bring to the boil. Reduce the heat to low and simmer for 1 hour or until sauce has thickened. Cool.

Preheat the oven to 190°C.

Cook the gnocchi in a saucepan of boiling salted water according to packet instructions. Drain, then toss in a little olive oil.

Divide the lamb mixture among 6 x 400ml ovenproof dishes and cover the top of each with gnocchi. Brush the tops with the melted butter, then sprinkle with parmesan. Bake the pies for 20 minutes or until golden. **Serves 6**

Lamb cutlets with Moroccan beans

3 tbs chermoula paste*

2 tbs olive oil

12 lamb cutlets

1 onion, finely chopped

2 x 400g cans borlotti beans, drained, rinsed

3 tbs honey

½ cup (125ml) vegetable stock

2 tbs chopped coriander leaves

Thick Greek-style yoghurt, to serve

Combine 1 tablespoon of the chermoula with 1 tablespoon of the oil. Toss the lamb in the mixture to coat and set aside.

Heat the remaining oil in a frypan over medium heat. Add the onion and cook, stirring, for 2–3 minutes until beginning to soften. Add the remaining 2 tablespoons of chermoula and stir briefly until fragrant, then add the beans, honey and stock. Simmer for 5 minutes until slightly thickened. Keep warm.

Preheat a barbecue or chargrill pan to high. Cook the lamb cutlets for 1–2 minutes each side until browned but still pink in the centre.

Divide the beans among 4 serving plates, then top with the lamb cutlets and serve with coriander and yoghurt. **Serves 4**

* Chermoula (a North African herb and spice paste) is available from delis and gourmet shops.

Homestyle meatloaf

3 cups (210g) fresh
  breadcrumbs
½ cup (125ml) milk
500g lean beef mince
500g lean pork mince
1 onion, grated
1 tsp finely grated lemon zest
3 garlic cloves, crushed
1 roasted capsicum (or use
  170g ready-roasted
  capsicum slices*), chopped
2 tbs chopped oregano
  leaves, plus whole leaves
  to garnish
¼ cup finely chopped flat-leaf
  parsley
2 tbs tomato sauce
1 tbs Worcestershire sauce
2 eggs, plus 1 extra yolk
400g can cherry tomatoes*

Preheat the oven to 170°C and lightly grease a 22cm x 14cm loaf pan or terrine. Soak the crumbs in the milk for 10 minutes.

Place the soaked crumbs in a large bowl with the remaining ingredients (except the tomatoes). Season with salt and pepper, then mix well with your hands to combine. Pack the mixture into the loaf pan and smooth the top. Cover with a piece of baking paper, then foil. Place on a baking tray and bake for 45 minutes, then cook uncovered for a further 15 minutes to brown the top.

Remove from the oven, then carefully drain any liquid from the pan into a saucepan. Cover the meatloaf loosely with foil to keep warm.

Add the cherry tomatoes to the saucepan, season with salt and pepper and bring to the boil. Simmer over medium-low heat for 10 minutes until sauce has thickened.

Place the meatloaf on a serving platter, pour over the tomato sauce and serve garnished with oregano leaves. **Serves 4–6**

* Ready-roasted capsicum slices are available from supermarkets. Canned cherry tomatoes are available from delis.

Minute steaks with pan-fried potatoes

1 garlic clove, finely chopped

2 tbs chopped oregano
leaves

2 tbs olive oil

4 x 120g minute steaks

Steamed green beans,
to serve

Pan-fried potatoes

4 potatoes (such as pontiac
or King Edward), peeled,
cut into 2cm cubes

2 tbs olive oil

Herb butter

125g butter, room
temperature

2 tbs parsley, chopped

1 tbs dill, chopped

1 tbs tarragon, chopped

1 tsp Dijon mustard seeds

To make the herb butter, whiz all the ingredients in a food processor to combine. Spoon onto plastic wrap, then shape into a log and enclose. Freeze until firm.

For the pan-fried potatoes, place the potato in a saucepan of cold, salted water. Bring to the boil over medium-high heat and cook for 3 minutes to par-boil. Drain and return to the warm pan, then cover with a lid and shake the saucepan to fluff up the surface of the potato. Place oil in a frypan over medium-high heat. Once hot, add the potato to the frypan, season, then cook, turning, for 8–10 minutes until crisp and golden.

Meanwhile, combine the garlic, oregano and oil in a small bowl and season, then brush over the steaks.

Place a chargrill pan or frypan over high heat. Once the pan is hot, cook the steaks in 2 batches, for 30 seconds each side or until just cooked.

Divide the steaks among plates, drizzle with any pan juices and top with some herb butter. Serve with pan-fried potatoes and green beans. **Serves 4**

New beef stroganoff

4 x 180g beef fillet steaks

¼ cup (60ml) olive oil, plus
   extra to brush

2 tbs mixed dried
   peppercorns, crushed

250g Swiss brown
   mushrooms, sliced

2 tbs brandy

1¼ cups (310ml) beef stock

1 tbs Dijon mustard

¼ cup chopped flat-leaf
   parsley, plus extra to serve

½ cup (125ml) thickened
   cream

400g pappardelle
   or fettuccine

Brush the steaks with a little oil, then season with salt. Sprinkle all over with the crushed peppercorns, gently pressing into the steaks. Heat 1 tablespoon oil in a frypan over medium-high heat. Add the steaks and cook for 2–3 minutes each side until well seared but still rare in the centre (or until cooked to your liking). Set aside and cover loosely with foil to keep warm.

Add the remaining oil to the steak pan. Add mushrooms and cook, stirring, for 3 minutes until they start to soften. Add the brandy and stock, then bring to the boil. Decrease the heat to medium-low and simmer for 5 minutes or until reduced by half. Stir in the mustard, parsley and cream. Cook for a further minute, stirring, until heated through.

Meanwhile, cook the pasta in a saucepan of boiling salted water according to packet instructions. Drain, then add to the pan with the sauce and toss to combine.

Slice the steak 1cm thick on an angle, then divide among plates with the pasta. Drizzle with any sauce left in the pan, then serve garnished with parsley. **Serves 4**

Steak fajitas with harissa mayonnaise

1kg piece skirt steak

1 bunch coriander

3 garlic cloves, finely
   chopped

3½ tbs harissa*

100ml extra virgin olive oil

1½ cups (450g) whole-egg
   mayonnaise

Flour tortillas, to serve

Salsa

4 cobs corn, cooked,
   kernels sliced

2 avocados, chopped

1 red onion, finely chopped

1 roasted red capsicum*,
   chopped

Finely grated zest and juice
   of 2 limes

Lightly score the steak on both sides. Finely chop the coriander stalks, reserving the leaves, then place the stalks in a bowl with the garlic, 2 tablespoons harissa and ¼ cup (60ml) oil. Season, then rub all over the steak. Cover, then marinate in the fridge for 3–4 hours.

Meanwhile, place the mayonnaise and remaining 1½ tablespoons harissa in a bowl and stir to combine. Keep chilled until ready to serve.

Roughly chop the reserved coriander leaves and place in a separate bowl with the corn kernels, avocado, onion, capsicum, lime zest and juice and remaining 2 tablespoons olive oil. Season, then toss well to combine.

Preheat a barbecue or chargrill pan over medium-high heat. Cook the steak for 3–4 minutes each side until charred, but still rare in the centre. Rest in a warm spot for 10 minutes.

Meanwhile, enclose the tortillas in foil and warm on the barbecue or in the chargrill pan.

Spread some harissa mayonnaise on each tortilla. Slice the steak, then divide among the tortillas and serve with the corn salsa.

Serves 6

* Harissa is a North African chilli paste available from Middle Eastern and gourmet food shops. Roasted red capsicum is available from delis.

Prawn, chilli & pesto pizza

10 green prawns, peeled,
deveined, chopped
2 tbs olive oil
2 garlic cloves, crushed
¼ tsp dried chilli flakes
2 woodfired pizza bases*
⅓ cup good-quality tomato
pasta sauce or tomato
passata (sugo)*
100g shredded mozzarella
or pizza cheese*
10 cherry tomatoes, halved
2 tbs pesto*, to serve

Place the prawn meat in a bowl with the olive oil, garlic and chilli. Toss to combine, then set aside.

Preheat the oven to 220°C (or heat a pizza maker on 2½). Spread the bases with the pizza sauce and scatter with cheese.

Arrange the tomato, cut-side up, over the base, then scatter over the prawn mixture, including the oil.

Cook the pizzas for 6 minutes or until the prawns are just cooked, the cheese is bubbling and the bases are crisp.

Serve drizzled with pesto. **Makes 2 pizzas**

* Woodfired pizza bases, passata and pizza cheese are available from supermarkets and delis. Good-quality pesto is available from delis; alternatively see recipe, p 18.

Spanish mussels with chorizo

2 tbs olive oil

1 onion, sliced

1 chorizo sausage, peeled,
  chopped

1 tsp smoked paprika
  (pimenton)

3 garlic cloves, finely
  chopped

¼ tsp saffron threads

400g can chopped tomatoes

¾ cup (185ml) dry sherry

2kg (about 36) pot-ready
  mussels

¼ cup flat-leaf parsley leaves,
  torn

Crusty bread, to serve

Heat the oil in a large flameproof casserole or lidded deep frypan over medium-high heat. Add the onion, chorizo and 1 teaspoon salt and cook, stirring, for 2–3 minutes until onion is soft. Add the paprika, garlic and saffron and stir to combine.

Add tomato and sherry and simmer for 3 minutes. Add the mussels, cover and cook for 3 minutes, shaking the pan from time to time, until the mussels open (discard any mussels that haven't opened after this time). Scatter with the parsley and serve with bread to dip into the sauce. **Serves 4**

Stir-fried prawns with Asian greens

3 bunches Asian greens (such
   as choy sum and bok choy),
   roughly chopped
¼ cup (60ml) sunflower oil
300g peeled (tails intact)
   green prawns, deveined
2 garlic cloves, chopped
1 tbs ginger, grated
2 tsp sambal oelek
   (Indonesian chilli paste)*
¼ cup (60ml) kecap manis
   (Indonesian sweet
   soy sauce)*
2 tbs oyster sauce
¼ cup (60ml) chicken stock
   or water
Fried Asian shallots*, sliced
   red chilli, coriander leaves
   and steamed rice, to serve

Blanch the Asian greens in boiling salted water for 30 seconds
or until wilted. Drain and refresh.

   Heat the oil in a wok over high heat. Add the prawns, garlic and
ginger, then stir-fry for 1–2 minutes until fragrant and prawns are
almost cooked through. Add the sambal oelek, kecap manis, oyster
sauce and drained Asian greens, tossing to combine, then add
stock. Cook for a further 1 minute to warm through, then divide
among bowls, scatter with shallots, chilli and coriander. Serve
immediately with rice. **Serves 4**

* Sambal oelek, kecap manis and fried Asian shallots are available
from Asian food shops and selected supermarkets.

Garlic prawn pizza bread

¼ cup (60ml) extra virgin
   olive oil
8 garlic cloves, bruised
1 cup flat-leaf parsley leaves
2 tsp grated lemon zest
450g fresh ricotta
½ cup (40g) grated
   parmesan, plus extra to
   sprinkle
1 baguette, split, or 2 large
   pizza bases
800g green prawns, peeled,
   halved if large (or 500g
   green prawn meat)

Preheat the oven to 220°C and line a baking tray with baking paper.

Place the oil and garlic in a pan over low heat and warm gently for 2–3 minutes to infuse. Stand for 5 minutes. Remove garlic cloves (reserving oil), then place the cloves in a small processor with the parsley and lemon zest and whiz until combined. Set aside one-quarter of the mixture, then add the ricotta and parmesan to the remaining mixture and pulse to combine. Spread the ricotta mixture over the baguette or pizza bases.

Place the reserved garlic oil in a frypan over medium-high heat. Add the prawns and cook for 1 minute each side or until just cooked through. Remove from the heat, then add the reserved garlic and parsley mixture and gently toss to combine. Arrange the prawns over the baguette or pizza bases, then sprinkle with extra parmesan. Bake for 5–6 minutes until the cheese has melted.

Serves 4

Hot-smoked trout & rice salad with mint pesto

1 cup (200g) long-grain rice

1½ cups fresh or frozen peas

2 cups firmly packed mint
leaves, plus extra to serve

½ cup firmly packed
basil leaves

3/4 cup (60g) finely grated
parmesan

25g pine nuts, toasted

¼ cup (60ml) lemon juice

1 garlic clove, chopped

1/3 cup (80ml) olive oil

2 x 150g hot-smoked trout
portions*, flaked

Cook the rice according to the packet instructions, then drain and refresh. Spread the rice on a baking tray to cool completely.

Cook the peas in boiling salted water for 2–3 minutes until tender. Drain, refresh and set aside.

Place the mint, basil, parmesan, pine nuts, lemon juice, garlic, ½ cup peas and ½ teaspoon sea salt in a food processor and whiz until smooth. With the motor running, slowly drizzle in oil until combined, then season to taste.

Toss the rice with the remaining 1 cup peas and serve with the pesto, flaked trout and extra mint leaves, to garnish. **Serves 4–6**

* Hot-smoked trout portions are available from supermarkets.

Cajun fish with corn & avocado salsa

2 tbs brown sugar

½ tsp each of chilli powder, ground cumin, paprika and mustard powder

4 skinless thick white fish fillets (such as blue-eye or coral trout)

1 tbs olive oil, plus extra to brush

Light sour cream, loosened with enough warm water to form a pouring consistency, to serve

Corn & avocado salsa

1 avocado, finely chopped

400g can corn kernels, drained

250g tomatoes, seeds removed, finely chopped

1 red onion, finely chopped

1 tsp sesame oil

2 tbs olive oil

1 cup chopped coriander leaves

Juice of 1 lime

Preheat the oven to 180°C.

Combine the sugar, spices, 1 teaspoon pepper and ½ teaspoon salt in a shallow bowl. Brush the fish with extra olive oil, then coat well in the spice mixture.

Heat the oil in a large ovenproof frypan over medium heat. Add the fish and cook for 2–3 minutes each side until golden. Transfer to the oven for 5 minutes or until just cooked.

Meanwhile, for the salsa, combine all the ingredients in a bowl and season to taste. Serve the fish topped with the salsa and drizzled with the sour cream. **Serves 4**

Singapore noodles

50g dried shiitake
    mushrooms*
2 tbs dried shrimp*
400g fresh Singapore noodles
1 cup (120g) frozen peas
1 tbs peanut oil
1 onion, thinly sliced
1 carrot, cut into matchsticks
1 red capsicum, thinly sliced
1 tbs mild curry powder
250g Chinese barbecue
    pork*, chopped
200g small cooked, peeled
    prawns
2 tbs Chinese rice wine
    (shaohsing)*
2 tbs kecap manis (Indonesian
    sweet soy sauce)*
4 spring onions, thinly sliced
    on an angle
Coriander leaves, to serve

Place the shiitake and dried shrimp in a bowl, cover with boiling water, then allow to soak for 15 minutes. Drain, reserving the soaking liquid. Halve the shiitake if large and set aside.

Meanwhile, place noodles and peas in a large bowl, cover with boiling water, and soak for 5 minutes. Drain, then gently separate noodles and set aside.

Heat the oil in a wok over medium-high heat. Add the onion, carrot, capsicum and curry powder, then cook, stirring, for 1–2 minutes until the vegetables have started to soften. Add the pork, prawns, rice wine, kecap manis, noodles, peas, shiitake, soaked shrimp, ¼ cup (60ml) reserved soaking liquid and half the spring onion, then stir-fry for 2–3 minutes until warmed through.

Divide Singapore noodles among bowls, then serve garnished with coriander and remaining spring onion. **Serves 4–6**

* Dried shiitake mushrooms, dried shrimp, Chinese rice wine and kecap manis are available from Asian food shops. Chinese barbecue pork is available from Asian barbecue shops.

Blue-eye with Spanish crumbs

2 anchovy fillets, drained

1 tbs capers, rinsed

Finely grated zest of 1 lemon

¼ cup (60ml) olive oil, plus
extra to drizzle

1 tsp Spanish smoked paprika
(pimenton)

2 tbs chopped flat-leaf
parsley

1 tbs toasted pine nuts

100g sourdough bread, crust
removed

4 x 180g skinless blue-eye
fillets, pin-boned

2 bunches asparagus,
trimmed

250g cherry truss tomatoes

Aioli (garlic mayonnaise) and
pan-fried potatoes with
chorizo (optional), to serve

Preheat the oven to 200°C.

Place the anchovies, capers, lemon zest, oil, paprika, parsley and pine nuts in a food processor and process to a paste. Add the bread and process to coarse crumbs (adding a little more oil if needed, to keep the mixture moist). Sprinkle 3 tablespoons of the crumb mixture on a baking tray and set aside.

Season the fish with salt and pepper, then place in a lined roasting pan. Divide the remaining crumb mixture among the fish fillets to cover, pressing in gently to form a crust. Spread asparagus and tomatoes around the fillets, drizzle with extra oil and season. Place the fish on the top shelf of the oven, and the tray with remaining crumbs on the bottom shelf. Bake for 10 minutes or until the fish is cooked through and the crumbs are golden.

Divide fish and vegetables among serving plates, scatter with extra crumbs and serve with aioli, potatoes and chorizo if desired.

Serves 4

Prawn, risoni & feta salad

300g risoni pasta (orzo)

1 telegraph cucumber,
peeled, seeds removed,
chopped

1 bunch watercress, leaves
picked

1 cup roughly chopped
flat-leaf parsley

1 fennel bulb, halved, very
thinly sliced (a mandoline is
ideal for this)

800g cooked prawns, peeled
(tails intact)

1 preserved lemon quarter*,
white pith and flesh
discarded, rind finely
chopped, plus 1 tbs
preserving liquid

1 cup (120g) pitted green
olives, sliced

150g feta cheese

2 tbs lemon juice

¼ cup (60ml) extra virgin
olive oil

Cook the pasta in boiling salted water according to packet
instructions. Rinse in cold water and drain, then place in a large
bowl with the cucumber, watercress, parsley, fennel, prawns, lemon
rind and olives. Crumble in the feta.

Whisk the preserved lemon liquid with the lemon juice and oil,
then season to taste with salt and pepper. Add to the salad and
toss gently to combine, then serve. **Serves 6–8**

* Preserved lemon is available in jars from selected supermarkets,
delis and Middle Eastern shops.

Simple kedgeree

300g smoked cod
1 bay leaf
1 tbs olive oil
20g unsalted butter
1 onion, finely chopped
10 fresh curry leaves*
1 cup (200g) basmati rice
¼ tsp garam masala
8 cardamom pods, lightly
    crushed
½ tsp ground turmeric
2 tsp good-quality mild curry
    powder
1½ cups fresh or frozen peas
2 tbs roughly chopped flat-leaf
    coriander, plus extra leaves
    to garnish
3 spring onions, sliced on an
    angle
2 hard-boiled eggs, quartered
Fried Asian shallots*,
    to garnish
Mango chutney, to serve

Cut the cod into large pieces, then place in a pan with the bay leaf and cover with boiling water. Cover and cook over low heat for 8 minutes or until the flesh flakes easily. Remove the fish with a spatula, then strain and reserve the poaching liquid.

Return the cleaned pan to low heat. Add the oil and butter, then add the onion and curry leaves and stir for 2–3 minutes until the onion has softened. Add the rice and stir to coat in the mixture. Add the garam masala, cardamom, turmeric and curry powder, then stir for 30 seconds until fragrant. Add 400ml of the reserved cooking liquid, bring to a simmer and cook for 10 minutes. Add peas and cook for a further 2–3 minutes until the rice and peas are tender, topping up with more cooking liquid if necessary.

Flake the cod into the rice mixture, discarding any skin and bones, then add the coriander and spring onions. Divide among bowls, then garnish with extra coriander, hard-boiled egg and fried shallots. Serve with mango chutney, if desired. **Serves 4**

* Fresh curry leaves are available from selected greengrocers. Fried Asian shallots are available from Asian food shops.

Baja fish tacos

½ tsp each of ground
   coriander, cumin, turmeric
   and chilli powder
½ cup (75g) plain flour
6 x 180g skinless flathead
   fillets
¼ cup (60ml) olive oil
12 small flour tortillas,
   warmed to packet
   instructions
½ iceberg lettuce, thinly
   shredded
½ red onion, thinly sliced
1 tomato, seeds removed,
   thinly sliced
Sour cream, coriander leaves
   and lime wedges, to serve

Combine the spices and flour in a shallow dish and season with salt and pepper. Toss the fish fillets in the seasoned flour, shaking off any excess.

Heat the oil in a frypan over medium-low heat. Fry the fish, in batches, for 2–3 minutes on each side until golden and cooked through. Keep warm while you cook the remaining fish.

Slice the fish into long strips and place in the warm tortillas with the lettuce, onion, tomato, sour cream and coriander leaves. Serve with lime wedges. **Serves 6**

Soba noodles with hot-smoked salmon and soy dressing

½ cup (125ml) rice vinegar
2 tbs finely grated ginger
1½ tbs soy sauce
2 garlic cloves, crushed
1 tsp sesame oil
¼ cup (60ml) sunflower oil
270g soba noodles*
2 cups (300g) frozen podded
   edamame (young green
   soy beans)*
2 x 150g hot-smoked salmon
   portions*, flaked
1 sheet nori seaweed*,
   cut into thin strips
2 spring onions, thinly sliced
   on the diagonal
2 tsp toasted sesame seeds
Micro coriander*, to serve

Combine the vinegar, ginger, soy sauce, garlic and sesame oil in a bowl. Slowly whisk in the sunflower oil and set aside.

Cook the noodles according to the packet instructions, adding the edamame for the final 3 minutes of cooking time. Drain and refresh, then place in a large bowl with the salmon and half the nori strips. Drizzle over the dressing and toss to combine.

Divide the noodle mixture among serving bowls. Garnish with spring onion, sesame seeds, micro coriander and remaining nori strips. **Serves 4**

* Soba noodles, edamame, hot-smoked salmon and nori seaweed are available from supermarkets. Micro coriander is available from farmers' markets and selected greengrocers.

Roast pumpkin & white bean salad

1kg butternut pumpkin,
    peeled, cut into 2cm cubes

100ml olive oil, plus extra to
    drizzle

1 tbs soy sauce

1 long red chilli, seeds
    removed, chopped

2 tsp honey

1 garlic clove, finely chopped

400g can cannellini beans,
    rinsed, drained

2 cups wild rocket

1 cup coriander leaves

Preheat the oven to 180°C. Line a baking tray with baking paper. Place the pumpkin on the baking tray, drizzle with the extra olive oil and season with sea salt and freshly ground black pepper.

Roast, turning once or twice, for 25 minutes or until pumpkin is golden and tender. Allow to cool slightly.

Whisk the 100ml olive oil, soy sauce, chilli, honey and garlic together in a large bowl. Add the beans, rocket, coriander and pumpkin. Toss well to coat in the dressing, then serve. **Serves 4**

Egyptian baked eggs

40g unsalted butter, plus
   melted butter to grease
4 eggs
1 cup (280g) thick Greek-style
   yoghurt
1 garlic clove, crushed
1 tbs chopped mint leaves,
   plus whole leaves
   to garnish
1 tsp hot paprika
Toasted cumin seeds,
   to garnish
Sliced toasted Turkish bread,
   to serve

Preheat the oven to 170°C and grease 4 ramekins or shallow ovenproof dishes with melted butter.

Crack an egg into each ramekin and carefully place the ramekins in a roasting pan. Pour enough boiling water to come three-quarters up the sides of the ramekins, then carefully place the pan in the oven. Bake for 5–7 minutes until the eggwhites are just set but the yolks are still a little runny.

Meanwhile, mix the yoghurt, garlic and mint in a bowl, season with salt and pepper and mix well. Set aside. Melt the 40g butter with the paprika in a frypan over medium-low heat. Stir for 1 minute until fragrant.

Place the ramekins on serving plates and drizzle with some of the paprika butter. Sprinkle with cumin seeds, and garnish with mint leaves. Serve with the yoghurt and Turkish toast. **Serves 4**

Mango & tomato curry

2 tbs sunflower oil

1 tbs panch phoran*

2 tbs mild curry powder

2 tsp turmeric

4 cardamom pods, bruised

1½ tbs grated ginger

1 long green chilli, seeds
   removed, finely chopped

10 curry leaves*

2 garlic cloves, finely
   chopped

1 onion, halved, sliced

2 mangoes, cut into bite-size
   pieces

6 tomatoes, seeds removed,
   cut into wedges

400ml coconut milk

Steamed rice, chopped
   unsalted roasted peanuts
   and coriander leaves,
   to serve

Heat oil in a wok or large frying pan over medium-high heat. Add spices, ginger, chilli and curry leaves, and stir-fry for 1–2 minutes until fragrant. Add garlic and onion, and stir-fry for a further 2–3 minutes until soft but not browned. Add mango, tomato and coconut milk, and stir-fry until warmed through. Season with sea salt.

Serve curry with steamed rice, scattered with peanuts and coriander. **Serves 4**

* Panch phoran is an Indian spice blend that includes cumin, fenugreek and fennel, available from spice shops, Indian food shops and online at herbies.com.au; substitute brown mustard seeds. Curry leaves are available fresh from selected greengrocers and dried from supermarkets.

Spiced carrot soup with coconut cream

1 tbs olive oil

1 onion, finely chopped

2 garlic cloves, finely
chopped

1 small red chilli, seeds
removed, chopped

1 tsp grated ginger

500g carrots, chopped

1 kumara (400g), chopped

4 kaffir lime leaves, 2 whole,
2 finely shredded

4 cups (1L) chicken stock

2 tbs palm sugar or brown
sugar

2 tbs fish sauce

Juice of ½ lime

200ml coconut cream

150ml thickened cream

⅓ cup (25g) toasted
shredded coconut

Heat oil in a large saucepan over medium heat, add onion and cook for 2 minutes or until softened. Add garlic, chilli, ginger, carrot, kumara, whole kaffir lime leaves and stock. Increase heat to high and bring to the boil, then reduce heat to medium-low and simmer for 20–25 minutes until vegetables are tender.

Remove kaffir lime leaves and discard. Set aside mixture in saucepan to cool slightly. Using a blender or stick blender, blend soup to a smooth puree, then return to the pan over medium-low heat. Add palm sugar, fish sauce, lime juice and half the coconut cream, then stir to combine.

Meanwhile, using electric beaters or a balloon whisk, whisk together the thickened cream and remaining 100ml coconut cream to soft peaks.

To serve, ladle soup into bowls, then swirl through a spoonful of the coconut cream mixture. Top with shredded kaffir lime and toasted shredded coconut. **Serves 4–6**

Salad of toasted sesame rice, edamame & mushrooms

1¼ tbs sesame oil

1 cup (200g) basmati rice

100g frozen podded
  edamame (soy beans)*,
  blanched, drained

2 tbs olive oil

1 leek (white part only),
  halved lengthways, thinly
  sliced

1 celery stalk, finely chopped

100g shiitake mushrooms*,
  sliced

2 spring onions, thinly sliced
  on an angle

1 tbs linseeds (flaxseeds)

1¼ tbs toasted sesame seeds

1 tbs light soy sauce

Juice of ½ lemon

½ tsp caster sugar

Heat 1 tablespoon sesame oil in a saucepan over medium heat. Add half the rice and cook, stirring, for 5 minutes or until toasted. Add remaining rice and 650ml cold water. Bring to a simmer, then cook for 7 minutes. Remove from heat, cover and set aside for 20 minutes or until water is completely absorbed. Transfer to a large bowl with the soy beans.

Meanwhile, heat 1 tablespoon olive oil in a saucepan over medium heat. Add leek and celery, and cook for 2–3 minutes until leek softens. Remove from pan and set aside.

Heat remaining 1 tablespoon olive oil in the same saucepan over high heat and cook mushrooms for 2–3 minutes until softened. Season well with sea salt and freshly ground black pepper. Cool slightly, then transfer to the rice mixture with the leek mixture, linseeds, half the spring onion and 1 tablespoon toasted sesame seeds, then stir to combine.

Whisk together soy sauce, lemon juice, sugar and remaining 1 teaspoon sesame oil and 1 teaspoon sesame seeds in a small bowl, then toss through the salad. Divide among 4 bowls and serve topped with remaining spring onion. **Serves 4**

* Frozen podded edamame (soy beans) are available from Asian food shops and selected supermarkets. Shiitake mushrooms are available from selected greengrocers.

Vegetarian chilli in avocado

2 tbs olive oil

1 large onion, finely chopped

1 tsp dried chilli flakes

½ tsp ground cinnamon

1 tsp ground cumin

1 tsp dried thyme

2 garlic cloves, chopped

1 tbs tomato paste

420g can three-bean mix,
   rinsed, drained

400g can brown lentils,
   rinsed, drained

400g can chopped tomatoes

½ cup (125ml) vegetable
   stock

2 tbs chopped coriander
   leaves, plus extra leaves
   to garnish

2 avocados, peeled, halved,
   stones discarded

Steamed rice, sour cream and
   corn chips, to serve

Heat the oil in a large frypan over medium heat. Add the onion and cook, stirring, for 2–3 minutes until softened. Add the spices, thyme and garlic and cook for 30 seconds or until fragrant. Add the tomato paste and cook for a few seconds, then add the beans, lentils, tomato and stock and bring to a simmer. Decrease the heat to low, then simmer for 15 minutes or until the sauce has thickened. Remove from the heat and stir in the chopped coriander.

Divide the steamed rice among 4 serving bowls, then place an avocado half in each. Top with the chilli, sour cream, black pepper and extra coriander. Serve with corn chips. **Serves 4**

White bean, coconut & lime soup

1 tbs sunflower oil

1 onion, chopped

1–2 tsp Thai green curry
    paste or jungle curry paste

2 x 400g cans cannellini
    beans, rinsed, drained

350ml chicken stock

2 kaffir lime leaves*

Zest and juice of 1 lime

400ml coconut milk

2 tsp fish sauce

Sliced red chilli, coriander
    leaves and chopped
    peanuts, to serve

Heat the oil in a saucepan over medium heat. Add the onion and cook, stirring occasionally, for 1–2 minutes until soft. Add the curry paste and cook, stirring, for 1 minute or until fragrant.

Add the beans, stock, lime leaves, zest and juice. Increase the heat to medium-high and bring to the boil, then reduce the heat to low and simmer for 10 minutes.

Cool slightly, then remove and discard the lime leaves. Puree using a stick blender (or puree in batches in a blender) until smooth, then stir in the coconut milk and fish sauce. Reheat gently over low heat. Ladle into serving bowls and sprinkle with chilli, coriander and peanuts. **Serves 4–6**

* Kaffir lime leaves are available from greengrocers and Asian food shops.

Stuffed field mushrooms with pesto

6 slices sourdough bread,
   crusts removed
⅔ cup (180g) pesto*
8 field mushrooms or large
   Swiss brown mushrooms,
   stalks trimmed
⅓ cup (80ml) olive oil
4 sprigs cherry truss
   tomatoes
2 tbs vino cotto* or balsamic
   vinegar

Preheat the oven to 180°C. Grease a large baking tray. Place the bread in a food processor and process until you have fine breadcrumbs. Add the pesto, season with salt and pepper, then process to combine.

Place the mushrooms, cap-side down, on the tray and brush with half the olive oil. Season, then fill each mushroom with some of the breadcrumb mixture. Arrange the tomatoes around the mushrooms, drizzle with the remaining olive oil, then season with salt and pepper.

Bake for 8–10 minutes until the tomatoes start to collapse and the mushrooms are tender. Drizzle with the vino cotto, then swirl the pan around to combine the vino cotto with any pan juices.

Serve the mushrooms and tomatoes drizzled with the juices.

Serves 4

* Good-quality pesto is available from delis; alternatively see recipe, p 18. Vino cotto (also known as saba) is available from Italian delis and gourmet food shops.

Greek salad frittata

10 eggs

2 tbs chopped flat-leaf
parsley

2 tbs olive oil

1 red onion, cut into thin
wedges

½ punnet (125g) cherry
tomatoes, halved

½ cup (80g) pitted kalamata
olives

100g feta, cut into cubes

Preheat the oven to 180°C.

Lightly whisk the eggs and parsley in a bowl, then season with salt and pepper. Set aside.

Heat the oil in a 20cm ovenproof frypan over medium heat. Add the onion and cook for 2–3 minutes until softened. Add the tomato and olives and cook for a further 2 minutes until the tomato begins to soften. Pour over the egg mixture, scatter with the cheese and bake in the oven for 20 minutes until the egg has set.

Leave the frittata to stand in the pan for 10 minutes, then slice and serve warm or at room temperature. **Serves 4**

Kumara galettes

2 small kumara, peeled, sliced
  into 1cm-thick rounds
1 tbs olive oil, plus extra to
  brush
375g block frozen puff pastry
  or 1 sheet frozen puff
  pastry, thawed
100ml creme fraiche or sour
  cream
100g Persian (marinated)
  feta*, drained
1 egg, lightly beaten
1 garlic clove, finely chopped
1 long red chilli, seeds
  removed, finely chopped
2 tbs chopped coriander
  leaves

Preheat the oven to 200°C. Line 2 baking trays with baking paper.

Place kumara in a single layer on 1 baking tray. Brush with oil and season with salt and pepper. Bake for 10–15 minutes until tender.

Meanwhile, if using a block of pastry, roll out on a lightly floured surface to a 24cm x 24cm square. Cut the rolled pastry or pastry sheet into 4 x 12cm squares. Prick in several places with a fork, leaving a 2cm border. Place on the second baking tray and chill for 10 minutes.

Spread the pastry squares with creme fraiche or sour cream inside the border and season with salt and pepper. Top with the roasted kumara, slightly overlapping, and crumble over the feta. Brush the pastry edges with egg. Bake for 25 minutes or until golden and puffed.

Meanwhile, combine the oil, garlic, chilli and coriander in a small bowl and season with salt and pepper. As soon as the pastries come out of the oven, brush with some of the dressing. Serve the remaining dressing on the side. **Makes 4**

* Persian feta is available from delis and selected supermarkets.

Index

The ABC 'Wave' device is a trademark of the Australian Broadcasting Corporation and is used under licence by HarperCollins*Publishers* Australia.

delicious. Simple comprises recipes and photographs originally published in *delicious. Faking It* (2008), *delicious. Quick Smart Cook* (2009), *delicious. More Please* (2010), *delicious. Simply the Best* (2011), *delicious. Home Cooking* (2012) and *delicious. Love to Cook* (2013)

First published in Australia in 2015
by HarperCollins*Publishers* Australia Pty Limited
ABN 36 009 913 517
harpercollins.com.au

HarperCollins*Publishers*
Level 13, 201 Elizabeth Street, Sydney NSW 2000, Australia
Unit D1, 63 Apollo Drive, Rosedale Auckland 0632, New Zealand
A 53, Sector 57, Noida, UP, India
1 London Bridge Street, London, SE1 9GF, United Kingdom
2 Bloor Street East, 20th floor, Toronto, Ontario M4W 1A8, Canada
195 Broadway, New York NY 10007, USA

National Library of Australia Cataloguing-in-Publication entry:
Little, Valli, author.
  Delicious: simple / Valli Little.
  ISBN: 978 0 7333 3364 4 (pbk.)
  Quick and easy cooking.
641.512

Author photo by Damian Bennett
Photography by Brett Stevens, Ian Wallace, Jeremy Simons
Styling by David Morgan, Louise Pickford
Cover and internal design by Hazel Lam, HarperCollins Design Studio
Typesetting by Judi Rowe, Agave Creative Group
Colour reproduction by Graphic Print Group, Adelaide SA
Printed and bound in China by RR Donnelley

6 5 4 3   16 17 18 19